The Adventures of
ARCHIBALD HIGGINS

COMPUTER MAGIC

D0851599

The Adventures of
ARCHIBALD HIGGINS

The Adventures of
ARCHIBALD HIGGINS
COMPUTER MAGIC

Jean-Pierre Petit

Translated by Ian Stewart

Edited by Wendy Campbell

William Kaufmann, Inc.
Los Altos, California 94022

Originally published as *L'Informagique* © Belin 1980
published by Librairie Classique
Eugène Belin, Paris

Library of Congress Cataloging in Publication Data

Petit, Jean-Pierre.
  Computer Magic.

  (The Adventures of Archibald Higgins)
  Translation of: Informagique.
  Summary: The curious Archibald Higgins falls into
a computer after keying a forbidden word and learns
how a computer works "from the inside."

  1. Computers—Juvenile literature. [1. Computers—
Cartoons and comics. 2. Cartoons and comics]
I. Title. II. Series: Petit, Jean-Pierre. Aventures
d'Anselme Lanterlu. English.
QA76.23.P4813 1985   001.64   84-21866
ISBN 0-86576-067-5

EVERYTHING YOU ALWAYS WANTED TO KNOW ABOUT COMPUTERS, BUT NEVER DARED ASK ...

5

13

14

15

16

17

19

20

21

25

BAG **4** CONTAINS THE FOLLOWING : ONE KNOTTED HANDKERCHIEF AND TWO UNKNOTTED ONES. IN THAT ORDER.

NOW FOR BAG **A** : TWO KNOTTED HANDKERCHIEFS AND ONE UNKNOTTED ONE — IN **THAT** ORDER !

WHAT DO THEY WANT ALL THEM 'ANKIES FOR, MAX ?

THEY'RE **BINARY CODE**. I SAW HOW THEY WENT ABOUT IT JUST NOW. THE UNKNOTTED HANDKERCHIEF MEANS **ZERO** AND THE KNOTTED ONE MEANS **ONE**.

AND THEN?

IT'S EASY: WHEN YOU COUNT, YOU WRITE ONE = 1, TWO = 2, THREE = 3, FOUR = 4, FIVE = 5, SIX = 6, SEVEN = 7, EIGHT = 8, NINE = 9. AND THEN, TO GET TEN, YOU PUT 1 AND 0 TOGETHER. THEN FOR ELEVEN, YOU PUT 11; TWELVE IS 12, AND SO ON...

THAT'S BECAUSE YOU'RE GIVEN **TEN** SYMBOLS 1, 2, 3, 4, 5, 6, 7, 8, 9, 0 TO CODE THE NUMBERS WITH.

$\int$ = $\emptyset$ = ZERO

$\int$ = 1 = ONE

BUT NOW SUPPOSE THAT YOU'VE ONLY GOT **TWO** SYMBOLS, INSTEAD OF THE USUAL **TEN**; AND THAT THESE SYMBOLS ARE $\emptyset$ AND 1 (*). INSTEAD OF **DECIMAL**, YOU'VE GOT TO CODE IN **BINARY**.

YES, BUT I KEEP GETTING **STUCK**!

(*) IN COMPUTING, ZERO IS WRITTEN $\emptyset$.

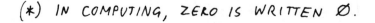

27

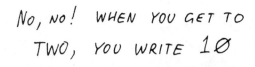

No, no! When you get to two, you write 10

...So three works out as 11. What do I do after **THAT** ?!?

BLIMEY, I'm getting the 'ang of this!

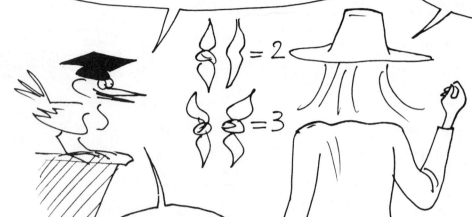

= 2

= 3

You show him, then.

Wot 'appens is that the contents of memory **A** is six — which is wot yer get if yer does the operation we was talkin' abaht — 2 x 3.

My word, now **THERE'S** a thing!

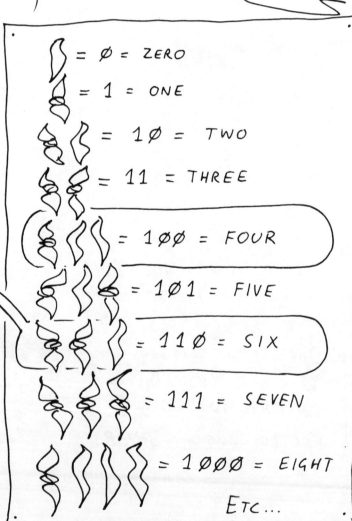

= Ø = ZERO

= 1 = ONE

= 1Ø = TWO

= 11 = THREE

= 1ØØ = FOUR

= 1Ø1 = FIVE

= 11Ø = SIX

= 111 = SEVEN

= 1ØØØ = EIGHT

ETC...

28

29

35

Sophie's Program

1	GIVE TO N THE VALUE ONE
2	GIVE TO I A VALUE AT RANDOM BETWEEN 1 AND 300
3	GIVE TO J A VALUE AT RANDOM BETWEEN 1 AND 300
4	FIND A(I), THE ITH WORD IN LIST A
5	FIND B(J), THE JTH WORD IN LIST B
6	FORM (BY **CONCATENATION**) M = A(I) + B(J)
7	PRINT N
8	ON THE SAME LINE, PRINT A SPACE AND THEN THE WORD M
9	ADD 1 TO N
10	IF N > 20 THEN STOP. OTHERWISE GO TO 2

EACH OPERATION, IN THE COMPUTER, IS IN EFFECT A MINI-PROGRAM. **ADDITION** AND **MULTIPLICATION**, FOR EXAMPLE, ARE PROGRAMS PERMANENTLY RESIDING IN THE COMPUTER. SUCH STRUCTURES ARE CALLED **SUBROUTINES**. WHAT WE'VE CALLED **CONCATENATION** IS ALSO A SUBROUTINE — ONE OF MANY AVAILABLE TO THE MACHINE. REMEMBER: $A(I)$ AND $B(J)$ ARE **STRINGS** OF LETTERS. CATENA IS LATIN FOR "CHAIN." THIS SUBROUTINE CHAINS TOGETHER TWO STRINGS OF LETTERS INTO A SINGLE WORD, WRITTEN SYMBOLICALLY $M = A(I) + B(J)$.

40

41

HELLO, HELLO, COME IN PLEASE! AH, **BUFFER**, INSTRUCTIONS 7 AND 8. PRINT OUT N AND THEN, ON THE SAME LINE, A SPACE, AND THE CONTENTS OF M.

OH, SUPER! MY PROGRAM IS RUNNING!

PRRRRRiiiiTT

1 COSMOPHOBE

COSMOPHOBE PRINTER

PAPER
STOP
TEST

MESSAGE RECEIVED, SIR! ROGER AND OUT!

COSMOPHOBE! THAT'S QUITE FUNNY. I'D BETTER THINK UP A DEFINITION FOR THIS NEW WORD THAT THE COMPUTER HAS "INVENTED". HOW ABOUT "SOMEONE UNABLE TO BEAR THE UNIVERSE"?

AT LINE 10 WE HAVE A **CONDITIONAL BRANCH.** IT'S BASED ON A TEST: WHETHER THE CONTENTS OF MEMORY N (WHICH ACTS AS A **COUNTER**) EXCEEDS 20, AND IF SO, TO STOP. IF NOT, THE PROGRAM GOES BACK TO LINE NUMBER 2 IN THE SERIES OF INSTRUCTIONS, AND CONTINUES — THAT IS, GOES ROUND ANOTHER TIME, DOING ANOTHER **LOOP.**

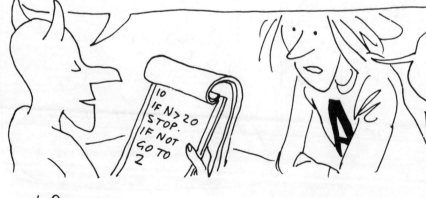

WHAT WOULD HAPPEN WITHOUT THAT KIND OF TEST?

10
IF N > 20
STOP.
IF NOT
GO TO
2

THEN YOU'D GET **UNCONDITIONAL BRANCHING**.

AND HERE THAT WOULD MEAN THAT THE PROGRAM WOULD GO ON LOOPING FOREVER, DOING THE SAME THING OVER AND OVER AGAIN.

OF COURSE, BECAUSE NOTHING HAS BEEN SET UP TO STOP IT. HERE WE FOLLOW ORDERS TO THE LETTER WITHOUT ARGUING. THE PROGRAM WE'RE WORKING ON HAS BEEN DESIGNED TO PRODUCE 20 WORDS; THAT IS, TO STOP AUTOMATICALLY AFTER LOOPING 20 TIMES. THE OPERATION "ADD 1 TO N" IS CALLED **INCREMENTING**, AND IT LETS US USE THE VARIABLE N AS A **LOOP COUNTER**. AND WHILE WE'RE WASTING TIME TALKING, VALUABLE MICROSECONDS ARE TRICKLING AWAY.

THIS IS WHAT HAPPENS WHEN YOU PROGRAM FIRST, THINK LATER!

I SHALL CALL THIS PROGRAM **THE LOGOTRON**.

17 CHRONOTHERAPIST: DOCTOR WHO BELIEVES THAT TIME HEALS ALL.

18 ELASTOLITH: BOUNCING STONE

19 MYCOCLAST: MUSHROOM-HUNTER

14 HEMIGAMIST ONE WHO IS HALF MARRIED

ORCHID?

43

A COMPUTER POSSESSES A COMPLEX RANGE OF INSTRUCTIONS, AND AN EXTENSIVE LIBRARY OF SUBROUTINES, THANKS TO WHICH YOU CAN COMPOSE A VIRTUALLY LIMITLESS RANGE OF PROGRAMS. HERE WE HAVE AN EXAMPLE OF **WORD-PROCESSING**.

AT THE MOMENT, COMPUTERS HELP US TO MANIPULATE DATA AND MAKE CALCULATIONS QUICKLY. IT IS HOPED THAT SOON IT WILL BE POSSIBLE TO MAKE COMPUTERS THAT POSSESS WHAT IS ALREADY CALLED **ARTIFICIAL INTELLIGENCE**.

THIS COMPUTER HAS STIMULATED SOPHIE'S IMAGINATION, BUT **SHE** IS THE MASTER. IN GENERAL WE CAN SAY THAT "THE COMPUTER CAN ONLY PERFORM THE TASKS THAT A MAN HAS INSTRUCTED IT TO DO, **AND NOTHING MORE.**"

BUT SOON, EQUIPPED WITH EYES, EARS, AND HANDS, IT WILL COMMUNICATE WITH THE WORLD **AUTONOMOUSLY**, AND TAKE PART IN ITS OWN EXPERIENCES, BEING ABLE AT THE SAME TIME TO MODIFY ITS PROGRAMS, THAT IS, ITS "WAY OF THINKING," TO IMPROVE ITS PERFORMANCE AND ITS ABILITIES.

PERHAPS IT'S THEN THAT OUR TROUBLES BEGIN...

OMNI

FINANCIAL TIMES

MACHIAVELLI
The Prince

TARSKOV MULTIMODAL LOGICS

VON NEUMANN THEORY OF GAMES

KEEP A CLOSE EYE ON THIS CHILD!

LEIBNIZ New essays on the HUMAN CONDITION

While Sophie continues quietly amusing herself, things are beginning to come to a head inside the computer...

46

47

ARCHIE AND MEGABYTE GO FULL-SPEED-AHEAD IN
SEARCH OF THE ERRANT MOLLUSC, TIRESIAS...

49

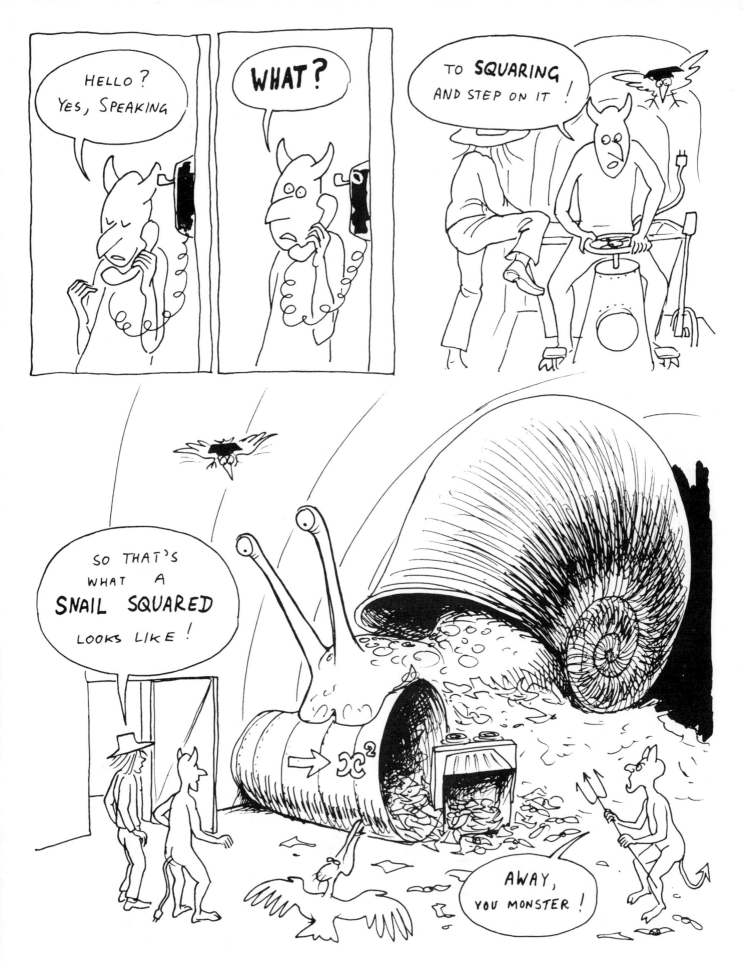

51

53

55

56

JUST NEED TO RECHARGE MY BATTERIES.

BETTER NOW?

YES. YOU WERE SAYING?

LET'S GET A FEW THINGS STRAIGHT. A COMPUTER, ABOVE ALL, IS AN **INPUT-OUTPUT SYSTEM**. THE ITEMS THAT IT DEALS WITH COME IN AT ONE END AND GO OUT AT THE OTHER. EVERYTHING IS CODED IN BINARY, BECAUSE YOU GUYS ONLY KNOW HOW TO COUNT UP TO **ONE**.

BY **INPUTS** WE MEAN SEQUENCES OF FIGURES AND LETTERS, TYPED OUT ON A KEYBOARD. IN **COMMAND MODE** THE **USER** TYPES INSTRUCTIONS AT THE KEYBOARD, IN HIS OWN TIME. THESE INSTRUCTIONS ARE THEN EXECUTED IMMEDIATELY (PAGES 15-30).

57

THE WORK IS PERFORMED BY HIGHLY SPECIALIZED **PROCESSING UNITS** WHICH OPERATE ON ITEMS THAT ARE CODED IN **BINARY** (HANDKERCHIEFS); AND THERE IS A NON-STOP FLOW (**BUS**) OF INTERMEDIATE RESULTS INTO MEMORY.

IF THE **INSTRUCTIONS** ARE PRECEDED BY A NUMBER, THE COMPUTER KNOWS AUTOMATICALLY THAT THESE ARE INTENDED FOR **DEFERRED EXECUTION**. THEY ARE THEN STORED IN THE **PROGRAM MEMORY**.

7 PRINT N

THEY ARE AUTOMATICALLY SORTED BY THE MACHINE; AND SUCH A SEQUENCE OF INSTRUCTIONS ARRANGED IN INCREASING ORDER IS CALLED A **PROGRAM**.

A SPECIAL COMMAND TYPED ON THE KEYBOARD TELLS THE MACHINE TO EXECUTE THIS PROGRAMMED TASK. THIS IS KNOWN AS **RUNNING** THE PROGRAM.

EXECUTE PROGRAM

IN PRACTICE THE INSTRUCTIONS ARE NOT WRITTEN AS ON PAGE 37. THEY ARE EXPRESSED IN A **LANGUAGE** APPROPRIATE TO THE PARTICULAR MACHINE.

THE RESULTS OF THE COMPUTER'S LABORS ARE PRESENTED WITH THE AID OF **OUTPUT DEVICES** (VDU*, PRINTER, AUDIO).

* VISUAL DISPLAY UNIT

STATODYNAMICS

STATODYNAMICS

STATODYNAMICS

SO, IF THERE ARE OUTPUTS — THERE MUST BE AN **EXIT** SOMEWHERE.

EXIT?

WELL, HECK, I MEAN — DON'T YOU KNOW WHERE YOUR INSTRUCTIONS **COME** FROM, AND WHERE YOUR RESULTS **GO** TO?

OTHER DEPARTMENTS.

NO, IT **AIN'T** UVVER DARNED DEPARTMENTS! IT'S THE DARNED **OUTSIDE WORLD**, MATE!

THERE **HAVE BEEN** SPECULATIONS ALONG THOSE LINES, OF COURSE. BUT IT'S QUITE IMPOSSIBLE. THINK OF THE **ENERGY** NEEDED TO TURN OUR COMPUTATIONS INTO PHYSICAL REALITY!

YOU'RE TELLING ME THAT — THAT ALL OF OUR CALCULATIONS HAVE SOME KIND OF **MATERIAL CONTENT**? A **PHYSICAL MEANING**?

INDEED!

59

65

67

69

71

BUT FROM THAT DAY FORTH, THE CENTER'S COMPUTER HAS SUFFERED FROM INEXPLICABLE BREAKDOWNS, WHICH NO SPECIALIST HAS BEEN ABLE TO CURE. PERHAPS THIS IS DUE TO ARCHIBALD HIGGINS'S **SHOE**, WHICH REMAINS INSIDE THE MACHINE — IN CONTACT WITH **EVERY** PART...

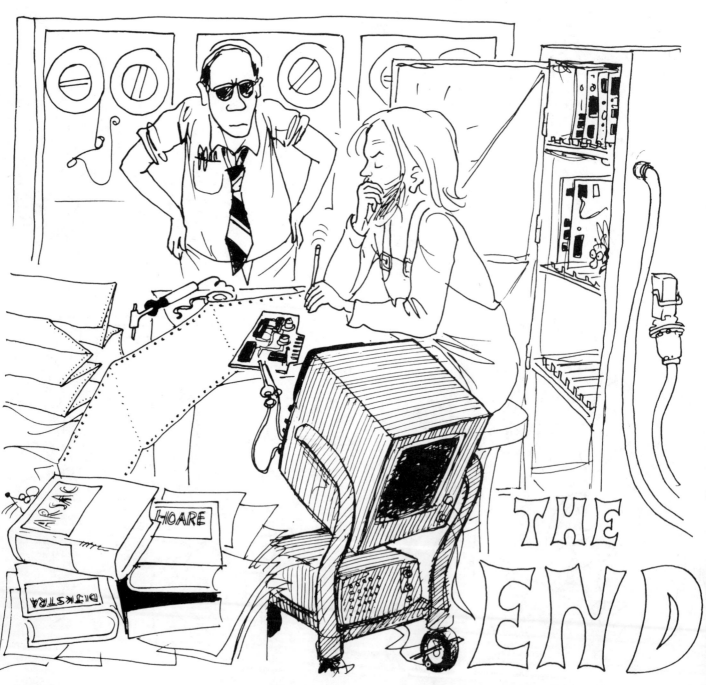